IMAGES
of America

MILWAUKEE
FIRE DEPARTMENT

In the finest tradition of the fire service, the Milwaukee Fire Department Honor Guard stands in tribute at the Staten Island funeral of New York firefighter Eric Olsen, who was killed at the World Trade Center on September 11, 2001. Flag bearers, from left to right, are: Michael Wojnar, Randy Leach, and Jeff Freiderich. (Courtesy Milwaukee Journal/Sentinel.)

(cover) With a good head of steam in its boiler, Engine Company 10's first-size Metropolitan steamer runs along downtown Water Street to a fire in 1916. Milwaukee's horse-drawn engines were pulled by three horses, either three abreast, or using a "spike hitch," with two abreast led by a seasoned horse. (Courtesy Milwaukee Fire Department.)

IMAGES
of America

MILWAUKEE
FIRE DEPARTMENT

Wayne Mutza

ARCADIA
PUBLISHING

Published by Arcadia Publishing
Charleston, South Carolina

Library of Congress Catalog Card Number: 2005924479

For all general information contact Arcadia Publishing at:
Telephone 843-853-2070
Fax 843-853-0044
E-mail sales@arcadiapublishing.com
For customer service and orders:
Toll-Free 1-888-313-2665

Visit us on the Internet at www.arcadiapublishing.com

This book is dedicated to my parents, Phillip and Lenore, and to my wife Debra's parents, Anthony and Wanda. Not only do they represent a sampling of Milwaukee's ethnic heritage—German, Polish, Italian, and Bohemian—they are, in their own way, a part of the city's history. The book is also dedicated to the 106 Milwaukee firefighters who have died in the line of duty.

CONTENTS

ACKNOWLEDGMENTS

A book covering the broad and dynamic history of the Milwaukee Fire Department is not possible without the help of many people, some of whom participated in the events that shaped the department. My heartfelt thanks to the following, who gave freely of their time and material: William Becwar, Wes Bernhardt, Tom Conrad, Mark Hoeller, Joe Kluck, James Koleas, Randy Leach, Chuck Liedtke, Chuck Pomazal, Judy Pomazal, David Tomasino, Debra Walsh, Dean and Sue Wassenberg, and Gregory Wenzel.

And to Chuck Madderom, who conducted much of the research for *Beertown Blazes*, an invaluable reference on the Milwaukee Fire Department; to the late Gerrit Madderom, MFD Battalion Chief, who harbored a keen interest in the department's history, and to his son, Brian, who proudly carries on the tradition.

To my brother, Dale; to Francy of Allied Digital Photo; and to Ron Zabler of Color Prints, Inc., for fulfilling my photo requirements.

To the legendary Gus Koleas, who not only wrote the afterword, but who enthusiastically supported my efforts more than a quarter century ago to initiate a program of preserving and presenting Milwaukee's fire department history. Today, that program exists as the Milwaukee Fire Historical Society, whose members, among their worthy efforts, operate the Milwaukee Fire Museum. My special thanks to the society's chairman, and MFD Captain, Jim Ley.

To the Milwaukee Fire Department and the Milwaukee Fire Bell Club.

And to my loving wife, Deb. Having met "on the job," we made a bit of fire department history ourselves.

MILWAUKEE FIRE HISTORICAL SOCIETY LTD

FRIENDS OF THE SOCIETY

INTRODUCTION

What comes to mind when you think of Milwaukee? Beer? Harley–Davidson? Machinery? Equally deserving of the recognition afforded these stalwart industries is the Milwaukee Fire Department, whose proud history was forged by the legions who passed through its ranks. Some have lost their lives, or were permanently disabled performing the noblest of deeds. All who ever held a nozzle, swung an axe, or breathed life into a victim laid the cornerstone for a department whose reputation is known across the country.

After it was incorporated as a city in 1846, Milwaukee's growth was marked by many of its buildings, including firehouses, built with cream-colored brick. The locally-made brick enhanced the city's architectural landscape, earning it the title, "Cream City." The fire department reflected Cream City's growth as the result of the influx of immigrants. This ethnic heritage, combined with the deep tradition of the fire service, enriched the department's colorful history.

In these pages you'll discover how fires, although thought to destroy history, have, in their sinister way, added their own pages to the historical annals. And you'll discover how Milwaukee's fire department earned its reputation as a leader in fire service, protecting lives and property in the great city of Milwaukee.

Submitted by the author during a department patch competition during the 1980s, this emblem symbolizes the face of Milwaukee, and the fire department's commitment to its citizens.

Members of Engine Company 1 pose with their 1861 Amoskeag steamer, named "Milwaukee," about 1870. Official uniforms were not adopted until a few years later. (Courtesy Milwaukee Fire Department.)

One

THE EARLY DAYS

Shown here is a rare photograph of one of Milwaukee's first pieces of fire apparatus. Buckets were hung along its wooden ladders, and both dapper firemen hold trumpets, undoubtedly the precursor to sirens. Note the dirt street, and a common type of Milwaukee establishment in the background at right. (Courtesy Milwaukee Fire Department.)

Jobst H. Buening was a chief of Milwaukee's volunteer fire department, taking office in 1858, until he was succeeded by 29-year-old Patrick McLaughlin in 1867. Four years later, Henry Lippert filled the position, to be recognized as the first chief of a paid, organized department. (Courtesy Milwaukee Fire Department.)

Chief James Foley was considered the most popular and respected chief of the MFD. He made vast improvements in the department, and he strongly advocated tougher codes to make buildings safer. He was appointed chief in 1883 and died, along with three of his firefighters, as the result of an acid spill at the Schwab Stamp & Seal Company in February 1903. (Courtesy Milwaukee Fire Department.)

HARPER'S WEEKLY.

JOURNAL OF CIVILIZATION.

VOL. XXVII.—No. 1361.
Copyright, 1883, by HARPER & BROTHERS.

NEW YORK, SATURDAY, JANUARY 20, 1883.

TEN CENTS A COPY.
$4.00 PER YEAR, IN ADVANCE.

THE MILWAUKEE TRAGEDY—DESTRUCTION OF THE NEWHALL HOUSE.—[SEE PAGE 39.]

This cover of *Harpers Weekly* captures the horror of the Newhall House Hotel Fire on January 9, 1883. Although firefighters rescued many occupants, more than 70 were killed in Milwaukee's largest-loss-of-life fire. As often happens in the wake of disaster, the fire was a call to action to improve fire department equipment and establish building codes. (Courtesy Author.)

11

At left is the cover of sheet music written by J.W. Kelly to memorialize the 1883 tragedy. (Courtesy Author.)

Hose No. 5's distinctive apparatus is pictured here, along with its equally distinguished crew, at Engine 5's quarters on Galena Street during the 1880s. (Courtesy Milwaukee Fire Department.)

This image shows a night run for a Milwaukee engine about the turn of the century. The motorized apparatus could not captivate the public as did a team of horses pulling a gleaming steamer belching smoke. (Courtesy David Tomasino.)

Seven steamers are visible, drawing water from a slip, in an early example of "drafting." During extended pumping operations, the horses were unhitched and tended nearby. (Courtesy Milwaukee Fire Department.)

Pulled by a trio of white horses, Engine Company 18 makes a run on Richards Street near its quarters at Richards and Clarke in 1908. (Courtesy Milwaukee Fire Department.)

In the driver's seat of this Amoskeag steamer is Engine 3's foreman, Henry Claymier, who three years later became chief engineer. Beards and moustaches were in vogue during the late 1800s. (Courtesy Milwaukee Fire Department.)

Fire horses were the department's pride; they were smart and had distinctive personalities. To ensure their health, in 1907 a "Horse Hospital" was built next to Engine 13's quarters at Nineteenth and North Avenue. Department veterinarian responded to all greater alarm fires. These animals were assigned to Engine 27 and Ladder 8 on Milwaukee's east side. The peak year for horses was 1912, when 250 were on the inventory. When replaced by motorized apparatus, horses were turned over to trucking firms or sent to pasture for their faithful service. (Courtesy Milwaukee Fire Department.)

During 1885, Chief Foley directed fireman Sebastian Brand, an ex-mason, to design new firehouses. Expert in architecture, Brand designed and oversaw the construction of more than 30 firehouses. He not only became superintendent of department buildings, but reached the rank of captain before his retirement in 1919. Typical of Brand's design was Engine 18's original quarters at Richards and Clarke Streets. A chief's Mitchell Roadster is parked on the cobblestone street. (Courtesy Milwaukee Fire Department.)

Engine House No. 8 was completed in 1883 on Seventh and North Avenue. Massive towers, used for spotting fires and for hanging hose to dry, were prominent features of Milwaukee's 19th-century skyline. (Courtesy Milwaukee Fire Department.)

The demand by Milwaukee insurance companies during the 1880s to protect valuables during fires led to the 1886 organization of the Milwaukee Fire Insurance Patrol, then called the "Sack Company." Total strength reached 25 men wotking in three companies, to protect property from fire, smoke, and water, before they were disbanded in 1940. They are still in use with fire departments as "Salvage Companies." Pictured here is Patrol Co. 1 during the early 1900s, on the run, and posed in front of quarters on Milwaukee Street. (Courtesy Milwaukee Fire Department.)

Engine House No. 4 at Second and Sycamore (later Michigan) Streets was one of a dozen firehouses built during the 1880s to keep pace with the city's expansion as a result of the influx of immigrants. Nineteenth-century firehouses adopted prevailing styles, their stately features reflecting the importance the city placed on its fire department. (Courtesy Milwaukee Fire Department.)

Led by an impressive team of matched horses, a steamer begins to work up a head of steam from its boiler. Shrouds fastened around the engine helped keep its intricate parts clean of road dirt. (Milwaukee Fire Department)

In an early example of cooperation between neighboring municipalities, the City of Kenosha presented this ornate banner to the MFD for sending engine companies to help battle a major Kenosha blaze on April 19, 1892. Just six months later, the Kenosha Fire Department would reciprocate, the first out-of-town fire department to respond with an engine and manpower to help fight Milwaukee's Third-Ward Fire. (Courtesy Milwaukee Fire Department.)

Pictured here are the ruins of Kissinger's Liquors on Water Street, one of 443 buildings destroyed in the Third-Ward Fire on October 28, 1892. The conflagration caused the greatest property loss in Milwaukee's history, engulfing 16 city blocks, along with 215 railroad cars. Three people, including a firefighter, were killed, and nineteen hundred people, mostly Irish immigrants, were left homeless. During reconstruction, Italians moved into the area, establishing grocery commission houses. "Commission Row" thrives as a trendy area, combining elements of past and present. (Courtesy Milwaukee Fire Department.)

Shortly after delivery, Milwaukee's first fireboat, the *Cataract*, lies alongside the U.S. Life Saving Station on Jones Island in late 1889. The *Cataract* was the first of six large fireboats used throughout the department's history. Their operational cost, a decline in port activity, and the diminishing riverfront grain elevators spelled the end of Milwaukee's fireboat fleet, which, for a time, was one of the nation's largest. (Courtesy Milwaukee Fire Department.)

Starting about the late 1880s, and for as long as horses were in service, some companies used sleighs to haul equipment through deep snow. If steam engines couldn't get through, hoses were hooked directly to hydrants. This was Ladder Company 7's sleigh, complete with alarm gong. (Courtesy Milwaukee Fire Department.)

Members of Engine Company 6 strike dashing poses with their steamer engine during the late 1800s. The inscription on the cylinder immediately forward of the huge boiler reads, "A.R.R. Butler," in honor of Ammi R.R. Butler, who served as Milwaukee's mayor from 1876 to 1878. Only a few companies were identified by both a name and number. (Courtesy Milwaukee Fire Department.)

To penetrate fires with a powerful stream from substantial heights, major cities used water towers, and Milwaukee was no exception. First purchased as a horse-drawn unit in 1889, the Hale tower was rebuilt by the department shop as a motorized unit, and underwent another rebuild in 1949–1950. It wasn't retired until 1967, having provided a record 77 years of service. (Courtesy Milwaukee Fire Department.)

Outfitted in the department's first official uniforms, the gang assigned to Engine 1's firehouse poses outside of quarters on Broadway during the late 1880s. (Courtesy Milwaukee Fire Department.)

Engine 7's steamer and hose wagons pose in 1881 in front of their first quarters, the former Bently School at Maple Street and Kinnickinnic Avenue. (Courtesy Milwaukee Fire Department.)

Members of Engine Company 2, with their Ahrens steamer and hose wagon, pose with the district chief at their new quarters on Fourth Street in 1893. (Courtesy Milwaukee Fire Department.)

The men of Truck 4 are shown here with their 1877 Babcock service truck, the only one of its kind used by the department. (Courtesy Milwaukee Fire Department.)

Two

1900–1920

Above is the snowy scene of the tragic Johns–Manville Co. blaze on February 13, 1909, which was billed as one of Milwaukee's worst fires. (Courtesy Milwaukee Fire Department.)

Steamers lasted well into the 20th century. This handsome 1883 Ahrens served Engine Company 18 from 1918 to 1921. It poses here on Engine 27's brick-paved ramp. (Courtesy Milwaukee Fire Department.)

Hidden at right behind all those men and horses in 1914 is Engine Company 2's Metropolitan steamer and hose wagon. Far left is Squadron No. 2, a manpower unit, with its 1914 Seagrave. Most of Milwaukee's first motorized fire rigs were purchased from Seagrave in Ohio. Boat Wagon 29 is at center. (Courtesy Milwaukee Fire Department.)

These photographs show the burning of the Johns–Manville Company at Third and Clybourn Streets on February 13, 1909. Many workers died, and six firefighters were killed when a portion of the building collapsed. Thousands of spectators were drawn to the spectacular blaze. During the following decade, greater alarm fires averaged 38 per year. (Courtesy Milwaukee Fire Department.)

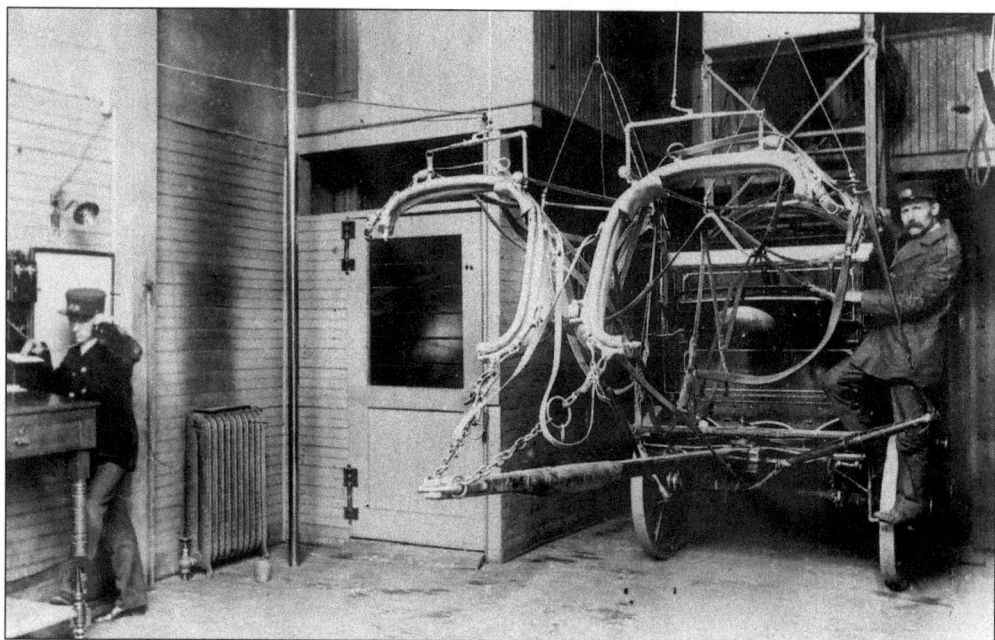

About 1900, an officer receives alarm information by phone as a firefighter prepares to hitch a two-horse team to the hose wagon's suspended harnesses. Flipping the alarm gong switch released the horses from their stalls. Old timers professed that horses could be hitched by the time the driver got to his seat. (Courtesy Milwaukee Fire Department.)

Pictured here are Chemical Company No. 8 and Boat Wagon 15 at their quarters on Elizabeth Street (later 438 National Avenue) in 1908. Boat wagons were stationed near waterways, carrying large hose which was laid as fireboats were en route. (Courtesy Gregory Wenzel.)

Engine Company 10's quarters on Broadway are pictured here during the early 1900s. The original firehouse was destroyed in the Third-Ward Fire of 1892.(Courtesy Milwaukee Fire Department.)

By mid-1990, 40 years after it saw use as a firehouse, privately owned Engine Company 10's quarters on Broadway had been renovated, complete with a statue of a firefighter and his faithful companion. (Courtesy Author.)

Three Milwaukee fireboats work at the Pabst Elevator B Fire on October 28, 1909. Water was pumped to land companies through hose lines visible to the right of Boat No. 15. (Courtesy Milwaukee Fire Department.)

Above are District Chief Henry Kruse and his driver, Robert Dallman, in 1911 in their Milwaukee-made buggy. Tradition dies hard in the fire service—today's chief cars are still called buggies. (Courtesy Milwaukee Fire Department.)

Firefighters work at a stubborn two-day fire on Grand Avenue (later Wisconsin Avenue) in Milwaukee's downtown. Smoke pours from the pumper's stack as it works to supply hoses with water drawn from a hydrant. (Courtesy David Tomasino.)

A pole frame with block and tackle was erected to right Engine 6's first-size American steamer following an accident at the intersection of Marshall and Mason Streets on Christmas Eve 1910. (Courtesy Milwaukee Fire Department.)

Temperatures well below zero didn't deter these Milwaukeeans from watching the action at the Bitker Department Store Fire at Eighteenth and Fond du Lac Avenue on January 12, 1912. When the fire was out, firefighters had to contend with equipment, including apparatus, frozen in place. This was the second of three major fires in the same building. (Courtesy Milwaukee Fire Department.)

The inscription over the doorway of Engine 8's quarters, "Chief Lippert No. 1," honored the chief of department Henry Lippert, and signified the home of Chemical Company 1, seen here with Engine 8 in 1907. (Courtesy Milwaukee Fire Department.)

The first motorized apparatus of the MFD were autos for the chiefs, beginning with Chief Clancy's Mitchell in 1907. Here, Chief L. A. Van Toor and his aide show off their 1912 Carter Car. The ratchet gong on the running board was a carryover from horse-drawn apparatus. (Courtesy Milwaukee Fire Department.)

Despite their popularity, only three American LaFrance units were purchased by the MFD in the early years. This 1916 example served as Engine Company 26 from 1917 to 1922. (Courtesy Milwaukee Fire Department.)

Milwaukee's first and only Ahrens Fox pumper arrived in 1915. Here, as Engine Company 3, the classic engine uses its front-mounted pump to draw water from a cistern. (Courtesy Milwaukee Fire Department.)

Chemical units carried bicarbonate of soda, which was activated by sulfuric acid to quickly control a fire before hose lines were laid and supplied with water. Chemical Company 1 shares the ramp with the first assistant chief's Mitchell auto at Engine 1's quarters in 1908. (Courtesy Milwaukee Fire Department.)

Bedecked with flags and firefighters wearing their parade best, Engine Company 32's American LaFrance participated in Milwaukee's Elks Carnival on September 10, 1920. The man seated at center wears a double-breasted uniform coat, indicating his rank as officer. (Courtesy Milwaukee Fire Department.)

Members of Engine Company 1 pose with their 1918 Seagrave at their quarters. The 750-gpm pumper was Engine 1's first motorized apparatus, serving the downtown company until 1926. Solid rubber tires, which weren't replaced by pneumatic tires until the 1930s, took their toll on both men and machine. (Courtesy Judy Pomazal)

Five steamers pump from a cistern during the Rialto Elevator Fire in 1911. Engine Company 9 is at center and Engine Company 21 at right. Elevators along Milwaukee's waterways accounted for many of the city's large fires until the 1960s. (Courtesy Milwaukee Fire Department.)

Three

1921–1940

Engine 14's 1921 Seagrave gets noticed by the driver of the steam engine, while his horses seem indifferent, as though aware of what motorization means to their future. (Courtesy Milwaukee Fire Department.)

Members of the Engine 27 and Ladder 5 of the 1920s pose with one of Milwaukee's first examples of a fire apparatus, a hand pumper built by A. Van Ness & Co. of New York. Through re-numbering, this rig was named "Milwaukee No. 1," and is one of two surviving hand pumpers. (Courtesy Milwaukee Fire Department.)

When this photograph was taken at the quarters of Engine 26 and Ladder 11, probably in the 1930s, firehouses were truly homes away from home. From 1918 until 1948, firefighters got one 24-hour period off every three days. (Courtesy Milwaukee Fire Department.)

An October 1927 edition of the newspaper *Milwaukee Leader* proclaimed, "This is the only city in the country that makes its own apparatus." The headline referred to 12 pumpers and 6 ladder trucks, along with 3 hose wagons, built from scratch by the department shop. The profitable endeavor lasted into the 1930s, with some of the MFD-built rigs serving nearly three decades. The MFD's ingenuity and resourcefulness were well known, as the department had built some of its own equipment since horse-and-buggy days. Truck Company 13's service truck (straight frame with no aerial) was one of six built by the department shop. Here, it rests outside its bungalow-style firehouse at Forty-seventh and Center Streets in 1926. Since most of Milwaukee's growth during the 1920s was in residential areas, these unique firehouses were built to blend in with neighborhood architecture. (Courtesy Milwaukee Fire Department.)

This scene is typical of January firefighting in Milwaukee. This was the St. Vincent De Paul Fire in 1940. (Courtesy Milwaukee Fire Department.)

The MFD seized every opportunity to educate the public about fire safety; these alarm boxes were demonstrated at City Hall Square during Fire Prevention Week in 1925. (Courtesy Milwaukee Fire Department.)

Putting out as much smoke as some of the fires to which it responded, Marine Engine Company 15 breaks ice in Milwaukee's Burnham Canal in January 1936. Milwaukee fireboats performed double duty as icebreakers during the region's frigid winters. (Courtesy Author.)

Two Pierce-Arrows were purchased in 1922, with this one converted shortly thereafter for use as Rescue Squad 1. The company had been established as Milwaukee's first rescue squad in 1919, to be followed by Squad 2 in 1927. Nearly two decades would pass before a third unit was put into service. (Courtesy Milwaukee Fire Department.)

Rescue Squad 2's right-hand drive reveals its early origin; it had been rebuilt in the MFD shop from a Seagrave combination hose/chemical car. It was then designated an MFD squad wagon, with an MFD logo on its radiator cowl proudly indicating its builder. Squad 2 handled all rescue work on Milwaukee's entire south side until 1942. From left to right are: Howard Thomas, Ted Medrow, Roland Brown, and William Wasichek. (Courtesy Author.)

Engine Company 5 and Ladder Company 3 are pictured above during the 1930s at their quarters at 1125 Galena Street. This pair recorded the most runs for most of their existence on Galena Street. Ladder 3's service truck was built by the MFD shop in 1930. As conditions improved over the years, engine companies were reduced to a crew of four or five, with ladder companies assigned five people. (Courtesy Milwaukee Fire Department.)

A 1920s-era engine pumps water to hose lines at a major blaze during the late 1930s. (Courtesy Milwaukee Fire Department.)

Milwaukee's Truck Company 1 is shown here in 1922. Delivered in 1909 as a LaFrance 85-foot aerial, the rig was pulled by a motor tractor beginning in 1913, and finally by this 1921 Seagrave tractor, which previously had been a hose/chemical car. Such reworking spoke volumes about the shop's capabilities, which provided the city nearly two decades of service from the truck. (Courtesy Milwaukee Fire Department.)

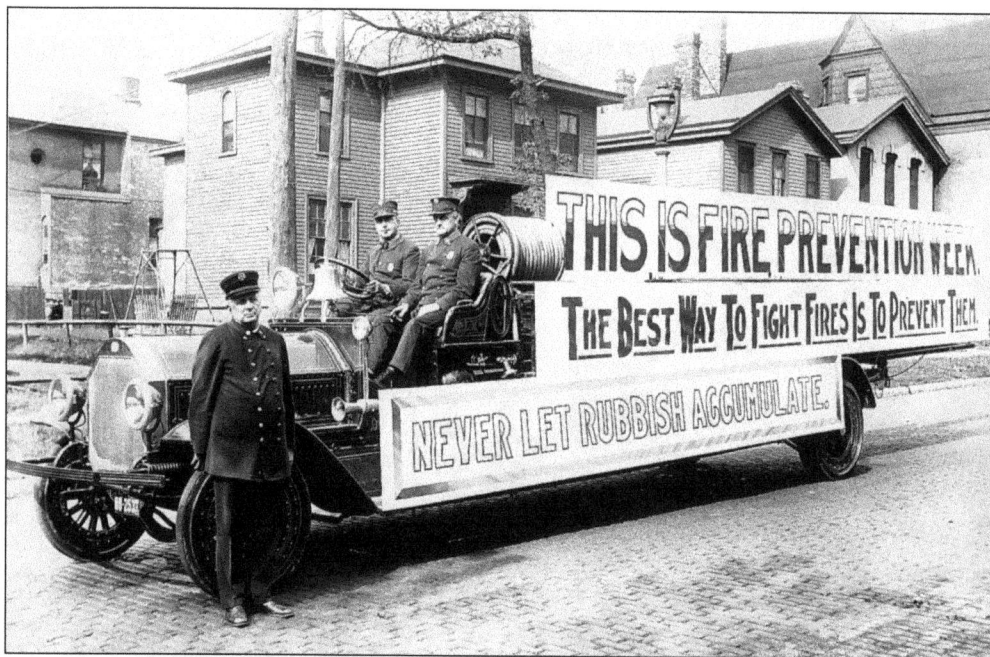

Beginning with its inception in 1915, Milwaukee's Fire Prevention Bureau went to great lengths to convey its message to the public. The activities during October's Fire Prevention Week included turning apparatus into billboards pleading fire safety. This image of a Seagrave truck and the battalion chief standing nearby was captured in 1922.

Yet another of Milwaukee's experiments with a one-of-a-kind fire apparatus was "Maggie," a German-built Magirus aerial, seen here demonstrating the lifting ability of its 100-foot aerial at Mitchell Park on July 11, 1928. Powered aerials were catching on, and Maggie's popularity was enhanced by the fact that her aerial could be fully raised in 30 seconds. Maggie went into service as Truck Company No. 1 (Courtesy Milwaukee Fire Department.)

A fire victim is taken down an aerial from the fourth floor of the Justrite Company on East Water Street on March 9, 1927. Undoubtedly, the fireworks sign on the building caused anxious moments for firefighters as they arrived. (Courtesy Milwaukee Fire Department.)

New Seagrave pumpers undergo tests at the Milwaukee River near the Broadway Bridge in August 1921. Grain elevators lining the river, such as the Rialto complex seen here, put the department to the test when they burned. (Courtesy Milwaukee Fire Department.)

With its firefighting equipment removed and alarm boxes placed in the hose bed, this engine took the important message of fire prevention to the public in the 1930s. The firefighter seems to have captured the attention of school children in demonstrating how to use alarm boxes. (Courtesy Milwaukee Fire Department.)

Chemical No. 1's Pierce-Arrow is pictured here about 1930. From left to right are: Joseph Ehms, Adam Pokrzywinski, and George Twinem. In the background is the county jail, which abutted Engine 1's quarters on Broadway and Wells Street. (Courtesy Judy Pomazal.)

The crew of Engine Company 7 is shown on the road with its new Seagrave pumper in August 1925. (Courtesy Milwaukee Fire Department.)

Despite technology, many aspects of fighting fires remain unchanged. Today, fire hose used in freezing temperatures is folded and carried on stake trucks as it was in this view on January 20, 1940. The temperature was a mere ten degrees when thousands of gallons of water turned the fire-gutted St. Vincent De Paul Society building into an ice castle. (Courtesy Milwaukee Fire Department.)

The year was 1940; however, the method used to clean fire hose was the same as today. Here, the members of Engine Company 5 scrub the "tubes" before hanging them to dry in the hose tower. (Courtesy Milwaukee Fire Department.)

This 1925 International fuel wagon serviced apparatus serving long-duration alarms. Municipal fuel trucks and the advent of diesel apparatus eventually eliminated the need for fire department fuel trucks. (Courtesy Milwaukee Fire Department.)

Milwaukee fireboats, such as No. 23, the *August Janssen* (above) did double duty as ice breakers to keep the Milwaukee River open during brutal winters. Milwaukee operated four fireboats until 1922. The following year the *Janssen* was sunk in Lake Michigan. The *Foley* met a similar fate seven years later. (Courtesy Milwaukee Fire Department.)

This ladder service truck was built by the MFD shop in 1930 and assigned to Truck Company 4, at Third (later Eighth) and Orchard Streets, where it served until 1946. Some ladder trucks, such as this example, carried chemical systems salvaged from older vehicles. (Courtesy Milwaukee Fire Department.)

Two fireboats enabled the use of powerful streams against fire in the Atlas Flour Mill at Commerce and Cherry Streets on December 10, 1926. (Courtesy Milwaukee Fire Department.)

The *Torrent* was Milwaukee's largest fireboat. Purchased in 1922 to replace the *Janssen* and *Foley*, she could pump 12,000 gallons of water per minute. The *Torrent* served 27 years before she was retired. Here, her deck pipes work on a coal yard fire as she supplies land companies with hand lines. (Courtesy Milwaukee Fire Department.)

Four

1941–1960

Typical of Milwaukee's experimentation with apparatus was "Maggie," purchased in 1928, when it was one of only three in the nation. Maggie was rebuilt four times, and served five ladder companies before being assigned to the training school. It is seen here working at a fire at Seventh and Wisconsin Avenue on December 26, 1946. (Courtesy John Hopwood)

This scene at Engine 1's quarters is timeless. The kitchen has always been, and continues to be, the hub of firehouse activity. (Courtesy Milwaukee Fire Department.)

Wearing canister masks—which were largely ineffective—firefighters enter the smoke-filled Myer–Eglash building on Water Street on April 10, 1956. More major fires have occurred along Water Street than any other in the city's history. (Courtesy Milwaukee Fire Department.)

Fire gutted the top floor of United Coal & Dock Company at Seventh and Wisconsin Avenue on May 10, 1947. Twenty-nine years later, the building was destroyed by a five-alarm blaze that threatened the main firehouse and fire headquarters a mere 100 feet away. (Courtesy Milwaukee Fire Department.)

Using portable ladders and their aerial, Truck 10's gang heads for the roof to ventilate as an engine company advances a hose line on the second floor of this burning home, about 1960. (Courtesy Milwaukee Fire Department.)

Firefighters advance hose lines up ground ladders as the water tower pummels the top floor of Hacks Furniture at Third and State Streets on November 29, 1952. This was one of numerous blazes in Hacks stores. (Courtesy Milwaukee Fire Department.)

Ladder Company 1's unique 100-foot Magirus was used to get hose lines to the top floor of St. Roses Orphan Asylum when it burned on April 3, 1945. The sanctuary, founded in 1848 and located next to St. Mary's Hospital on North Lake Drive, was one of many social welfare institutions established during the reign of Milwaukee Catholic bishop John Henri. (Courtesy Milwaukee Fire Department.)

Concern shows on the faces of firefighters as they assist a comrade overcome during a four-alarm fire at Twenty-fourth and State Streets on November 8, 1952. (Courtesy Milwaukee Fire Department.)

There's certainly lots of brass here. At this chief's meeting, about 1950, Chief Wischer (in suit) sits at the head of the table. The large pictorial roster at left is displayed in the Fire Academy office. (Courtesy Gustave Koleas.)

Truck Company 1's Magirus wears a liberal coating of ice after battling a four-alarm blaze on downtown's Water Street on December 18, 1947. (Courtesy Milwaukee Fire Department.)

A pair of MFD-built pumpers (Engine 3 in foreground) work at the United Coal & Dock Fire at Seventh and Wisconsin Streets on May 10, 1947. (Courtesy Milwaukee Fire Department.)

Firefighters of Engine Company 30 welcome a new 1949 Mack pumper as a replacement for their 1921 Seagrave. The delivery signaled the beginning of a trend in Mack apparatus for the department. (Courtesy Milwaukee Fire Department.)

Using a mechanical inhalator, a member of Rescue Squad 1 administers oxygen to a firefighter overcome at a fire in 1946. (Courtesy Milwaukee Fire Department.)

Throughout much of the department's history, involvement in sports has played a part in promoting health, teamwork, and the competitive spirit. This is the MFD Baseball Team in 1945. (Courtesy Milwaukee Fire Department.)

More than 100 occupants of the Martin Hotel on Wisconsin Avenue and Van Buren Street were rescued, many by ladders, when a five-alarm fire broke out in February 1948. (Courtesy Milwaukee Fire Department.)

Besides daily housekeeping and equipment maintenance, specific chores were done on designated days. Here, it's Thursday, or "Kerosene Day," at Engine 1 in 1956. All vehicles were cleaned inside and out, the tougher grime removed with kerosene. Then there were "Brass Day," "Windows Day," "Ladder Day," and "Mask Day," with Sunday welcomed as "Holiday Routine." (Courtesy Milwaukee Fire Department.)

Using large-caliber master streams, Milwaukee firefighters endure frigid temperatures to fight a stubborn blaze at Meyer Stores at Eighteenth and Fond du Lac Avenue on February 21, 1955. (Courtesy Milwaukee Fire Department.)

This 1935 Mack tank truck, along with several other vehicles, was acquired through annexation of Town of Lake in 1954. Tank trucks provided water in outlying areas where hydrants had yet to be installed. (Courtesy Author.)

Engine Company 35 was first to arrive when two cars of the Milwaukee Electric Lines collided on August 24, 1949. Surprisingly, no one was killed, although many were injured. The accident happened at Fifty-second and Story Parkway near Soldier's Home on the city's west side. After a train backed up, a following train slammed into it. A major rail accident one year later caused ten deaths and many injuries, spelling the end of Rapid Transit in Milwaukee. (Courtesy Milwaukee Fire Department.)

The clock on City Hall in the background records 6:40 p.m. on December 18, 1947, as Truck Company No. 1 and the water tower (far left) add to the master streams used to fight a four-alarm fire at 1023 North Water Street. The City Hall tower itself was badly damaged in a 1929 blaze. (Courtesy Milwaukee Fire Department.)

Firefighters went to any length to promote fire prevention, and the department itself, including this dramatic demonstration during the 1940s. (Courtesy Milwaukee Fire Department.)

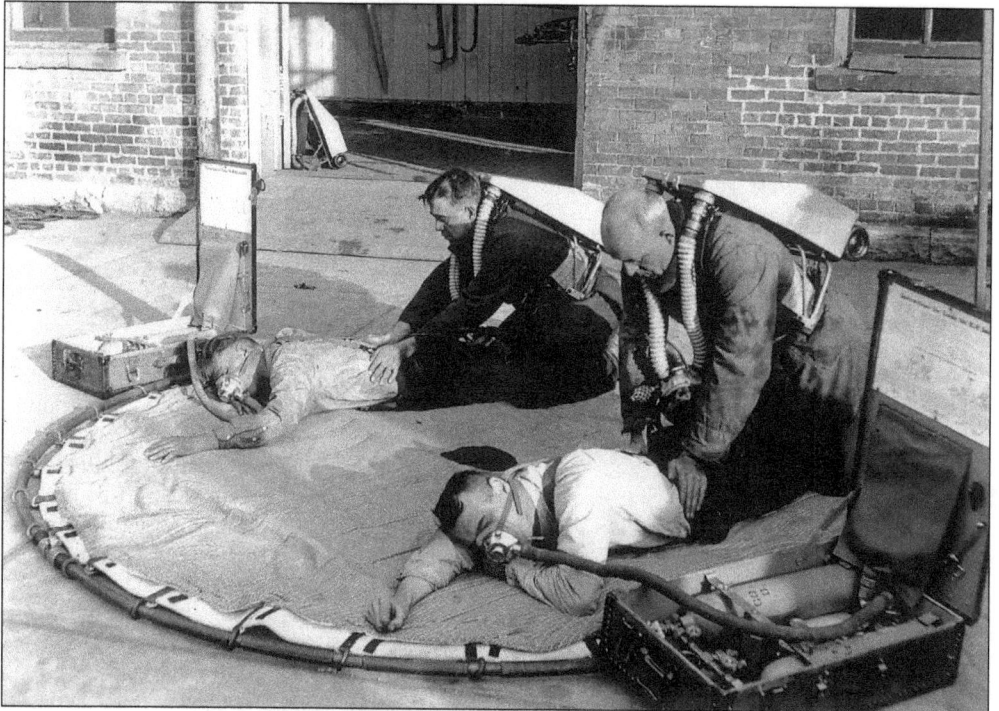

Since saving lives was paramount, the MFD continually sought new equipment and techniques. Wearing experimental breathing apparatus, these firefighters practice life-saving techniques using mechanical respirators during the 1940s. (Courtesy Milwaukee Fire Department.)

Truck Company 2's 1942 Pirsch aerial doubles as a water tower at Pittsburgh Plate Glass on June 12, 1946. The three-alarm blaze at the paint manufacturer produced multi-colored smoke. Two dozen firefighters were overcome by smoke and fumes. (Courtesy Milwaukee Fire Department.)

Edward E. Wischer served as department chief from 1945 to 1959. Wischer saw the department through post-World War II recovery, and he faced the department's first struggle with manpower reductions. (Courtesy Milwaukee Fire Department.)

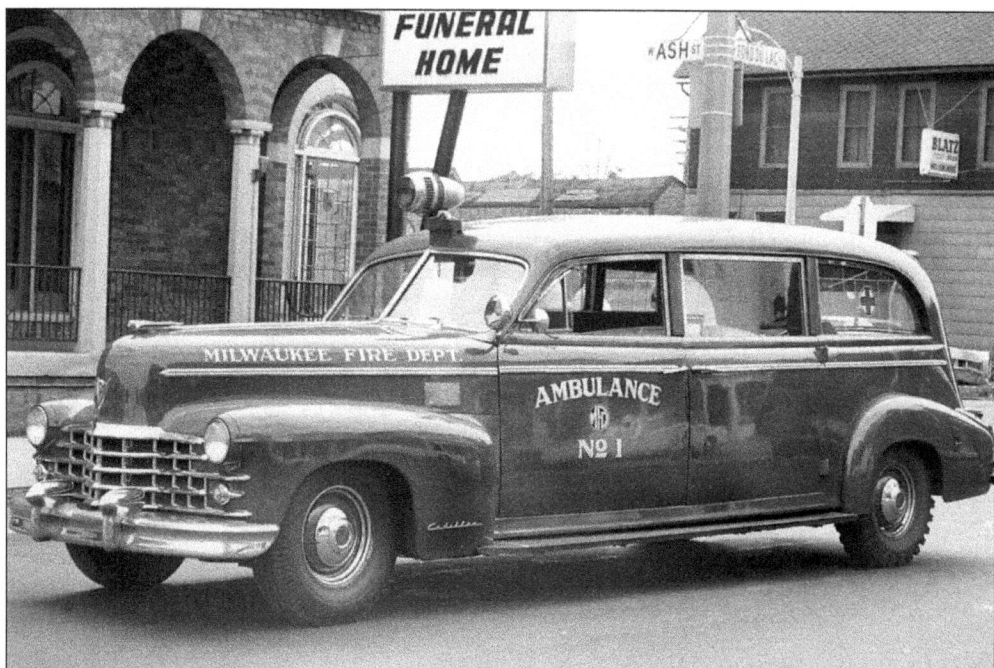

Ambulance No. 1 was a 1947 Cadillac purchased by the Milwaukee Fire Bell Club and donated to the department. When it was retired during the 1970s, it was in pristine condition, and had few miles, making it the envy of car enthusiasts. (Courtesy Author.)

The massive body of this 1942 GMC rescue squad was built by Milwaukee's Barkow Company. Rescue scenes were hand-painted on its sides. (Courtesy Milwaukee Fire Department.)

Although curbs were placed on fire department equipment purchases, there were plenty of beer trucks in Milwaukee during World War II, some of which were loaned to the fire department for outfitting as fire apparatus. The MFD shop converted 31 civilian trucks with government-supplied skid pumps. At war's end, all firefighting gear was removed and the trucks were returned to carry on the business of taking care of a thirsty city. (Courtesy Milwaukee Fire Department.)

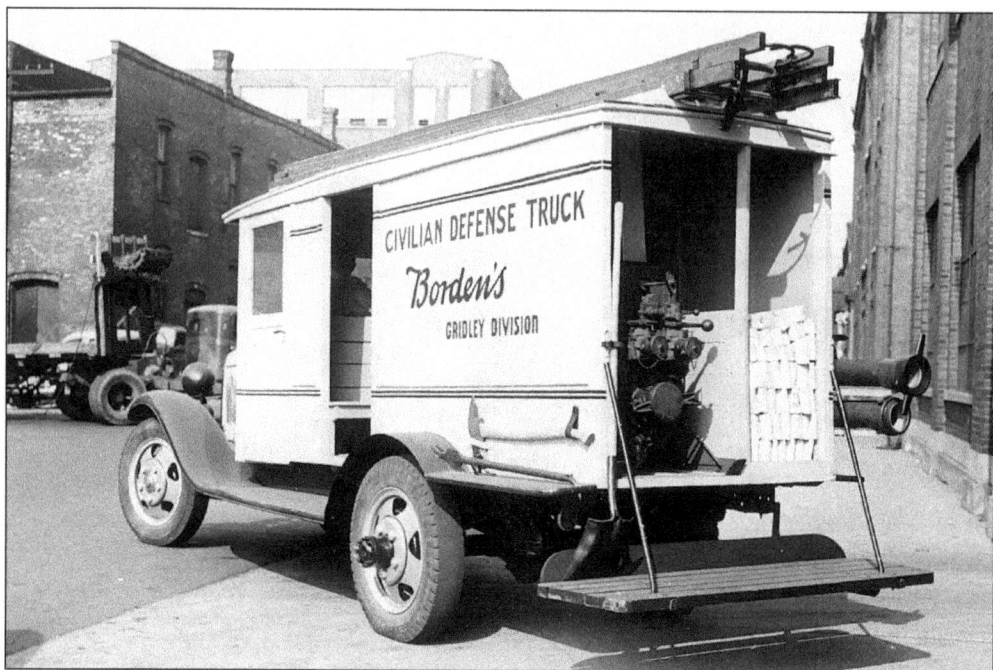

Not only beer deliveries were compromised during World War II. This milk truck was pressed into service as fire apparatus, to offset the curtailment of new equipment purchases, and as auxiliary defense equipment. (Courtesy Milwaukee Fire Department.)

As part of the war effort, the government in 1943 delivered 59 pump trailers to the fire department for auxiliary firefighting. Thousands of other pieces of equipment, including ladders, hoses, cots, and helmets also arrived by rail. To compensate for the equipment and manpower shortage caused by the war, more than 3,000 civilians were trained as auxiliary firefighters. (Courtesy Milwaukee Fire Department.)

Other than experimental vehicles, Milwaukee's first powered aerial ladders came from the Peter Pirsch Company of nearby Kenosha, Wisconsin. Pirsch aerials were made of aluminum, a trend the firm started in 1935. Truck Company 8's Pirsch was one of two delivered in 1942, the other having been assigned to Truck Company 2. (Courtesy Chuck Madderom.)

Wisconsin winters didn't seem to get any easier, and the 1947 blizzard that paralyzed the city prompted the purchase of two snow tractors from military surplus. Built by Milwaukee's own Allis Chalmers Corp., the multi-purpose vehicles were capable of traversing many types of terrain, from paved roads to steep snowy slopes. (Courtesy Milwaukee Fire Department.)

During the late 1940s, the switch was made to Mack engines, such as this 1949 example, which served as Engine Company 31 on Milwaukee's south side. All were eventually modified with side cabinets to accommodate breathing apparatus. (Courtesy Chuck Madderom.)

Rescue Squad 3 displays its specialized equipment in 1947. The unit was re-designated a special equipment truck in 1958, and was removed from service in 1974, when ladder companies began carrying specialized equipment. (Courtesy Milwaukee Fire Department.)

Engine Company 36's 1946 Pirsch was rated at 1,250 gpm. Apparatus built during World War II had little chrome in observance of restrictions governing the use of certain metals. (Courtesy Author.)

Among the MFD's purchases of one-of-a-kind apparatus was this classic American LaFrance pumper. It served less than five years before it crashed at the Hawley Road railroad crossing at State Street, only to be rammed by a train minutes later. Amazingly, no one was seriously hurt in the incident, which occurred on June 20, 1954. (Courtesy Milwaukee Fire Department.)

| 291 | 400 N. |
| W. ST. PAUL AVE. & N. 5TH ST. | 500 W. |

ENGINE		TRUCK	SQ.	BN. CHIEF
20- 2 · 3	B & H	2 · 8		1
1 -28-12		1 · 4	1	2
9 -21· 6		7		5
13- 5 -18		18		
32-24-26				
2ND ALARM TRANSFER				
13-30		12		
2 · 1		2		
3RD ALARM TRANSFER				
24-25		19		4
9 ·21		18		1
4TH ALARM TRANSFER				
32-37				
2 -13				
5TH ALARM TRANSFER				
36-22-23				
2 · 9 ·12				

Beginning in 1910, companies responded to alarms per "running cards," which were used until computer automation was introduced during the 1990s. According to this running card for Box 291, first responding units were Engines 20, 2, and 3, the fireboat, a high pressure unit, Ladders 2 and 8, and the First Battalion Chief. The next four lines indicate company responses for second through fifth alarms. (Courtesy Author.)

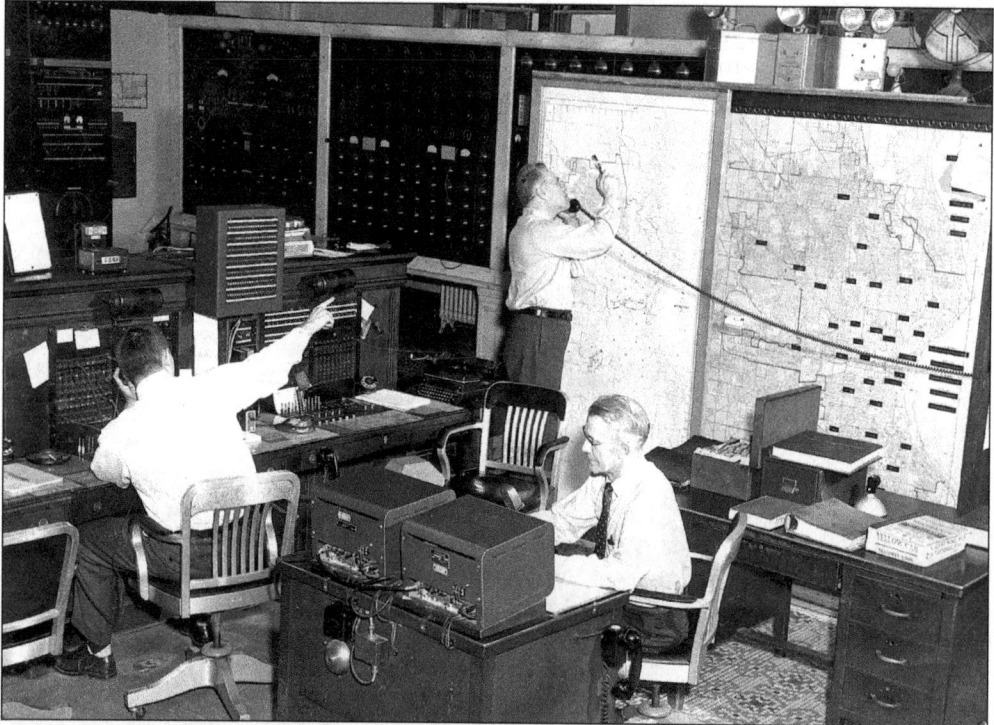

Milwaukee's fire alarm center began operations in 1869. For most of its existence it was staffed by non-active firefighters, and located in City Hall. This photograph, probably taken during the 1940s, portrays a highly effective alarm and dispatch system using rudimentary telephones, radios, and map plotting boards. Back-up power could keep the alarm center running, even if the entire city lost power. (Courtesy Milwaukee Fire Department.)

Firefighters, some wearing their helmets reversed as heat shields, struggle to reposition hose lines during this major 1940s blaze. (Courtesy Milwaukee Fire Department.)

Ladder Company 16's 1949 Pirsch with an 85-foot aerial was typical of the ladder trucks purchased by Milwaukee during the late 1940s and early 1950s. Strangely, especially in view of Wisconsin weather, apparatus purchased during this period featured open cabs, compared to earlier closed cab models. One explanation offered by old-timers points to a chief who insisted that officers be able to see the upper portions of burning buildings as they approached the scene. (Courtesy Gerrit Madderom.)

Most unusual among Milwaukee firehouses was this residence at Eighty-fourth and Morgan Avenue, which was leased by the city from 1956 to 1984 to accommodate Engine Company 29 on the south side. (Courtesy Author.)

Success with the 100-foot, four-section Magirus aerial named "Maggie," purchased in 1928, led to the purchase in 1957 of these three German-built Magirus aerials mounted on Mack trucks. They began service as Truck Companies 1, 2, and 18. An experiment a few years later with a similar truck style involved a Dutch-made Geesink aerial mounted to an FWD truck. (Courtesy Author.)

The crew of Truck Company 1 answers the alarm in 1957. The German-built four-section Magirus aerial was mounted to a Mack B-85 cab and chassis, whose short wheel-base offered great maneuverability in the downtown area. (Courtesy Author.)

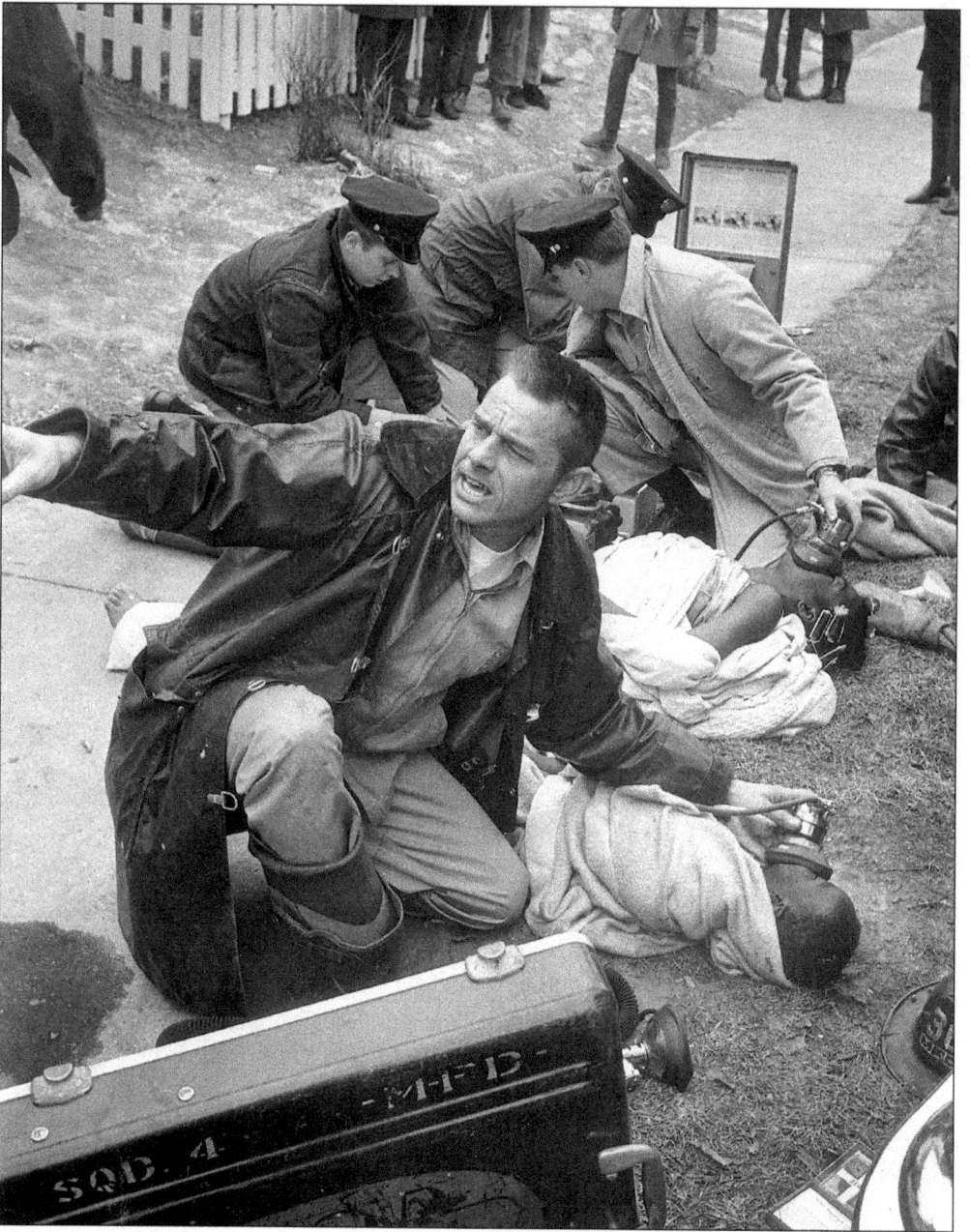

Milwaukee firefighters work to revive victims of a house fire at Fifteenth and Hadley Streets in 1960. One child died and six others were injured. (Courtesy Milwaukee Fire Department.)

Five

1961–1980

The water curtain from High Pressure 1 saved the building next to the downtown Robert Rom building when it burned on June 4, 1964. (Courtesy Milwaukee Fire Department.)

Members of the fire service agree that the most important advancement in their line of work has been self-contained breathing apparatus (SCBA). Here, firefighter Ronald Reinke wears the first type of SCBA used by the MFD. (Courtesy Milwaukee Fire Department.)

Firefighter George Aussprung prepares to enter the thick of things in a fire at the NAACP headquarters on North Third Street in December 1968. (Courtesy Milwaukee Fire Department.)

By the 1920s, Milwaukee had installed nearly 13 miles of fireboat pipeline as a means of supplying large volumes of water inland. Here, the fireboat *Deluge* taps into one of the special connections for a three-alarm fire at Canal Street and Muskego Avenue in October 1966. The 12,000-gpm *Deluge* was Milwaukee's last large fireboat, arriving in 1949; it fell victim to budget woes during the 1980s. (Courtesy Milwaukee Fire Department.)

Panel trucks used as rescue squads were replaced by vans such as Squad 5's 1966 Ford. During the late 1970s, federal regulations required the switch to larger vans, and, finally, modular units. (Courtesy Author.)

Feeling the effects of a stubborn three-alarm fire during the hot summer of 1973, firefighters take a well-deserved breather. (Courtesy King Monaghan.)

Throughout its history, the MFD has been faced with a wide variety of situations, some more unusual than others, such as this airplane crash on West Capitol Drive in 1973. (Courtesy Author.)

Firefighter/Paramedic Gregory Davis and Paramedic Officer Mary Horsmann treat a person injured in a house fire. Horsmann (then Polasek) and another woman joined Sue Bethke (now Wassenberg), who in 1977 became the first female to pass the firefighter entrance tests. None, however, passed the training. In 1974, a federal judge had ruled the exams discriminatory and ordered the department to devise a system for hiring women firefighters. Chief Stamm resisted, saying the department felt forced to hire physically unqualified individuals. Many felt that standards were being lowered. A proposed county-wide paramedic plan offered a solution, when it was ruled that women could become paramedics without passing firefighter training. (Courtesy Milwaukee Fire Department.)

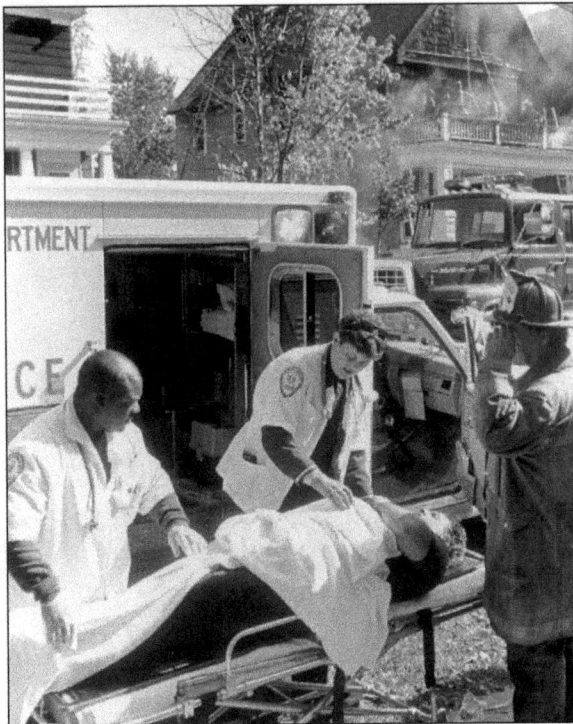

CITY OF MILWAUKEE
FIREFIGHTERS WANTED

ALL WOMEN, REGARDLESS OF RACE, & MINORITY MEN!

STARTING SALARY:

$15,518

DO YOU QUALIFY?

Apply now for a career in Firefighting. We offer qualified individuals a starting salary of $15,518, a work schedule of one day on, two days off, attractive vacation and sick leave schedule, full insurance program, and pension benefits contributed by the City. Accept a new career challenge; become a member of a proud service; be a City of Milwaukee Firefighter. Applications are now being accepted from all women and minority males who meet minimum qualifications. (Applications are not presently available to majority males because an eligibility list continues in effect.) If your age is 19 to 29, a U.S. Citizen and resident of Wisconsin one year immediately prior to filing, a High School graduate or GED equivalent, have excellent health, and possess and Unrestricted Driver's license, you are encouraged to apply.
Women are specifically advised that they are eligible to apply for Firefighter and all persons are judged on their ability to qualify on the basis of performance on job related criteria. This opportunity is available to assure representative hiring and the Commission is required by Federal Court Order to hire a significant number of Black, Hispanic, American Indian, and female persons.
Application forms are available at the Office of the Fire and Police Commission only, telephone 276-2400 for further details. Application forms will be issued and accepted in the Office of the Fire and Police Commission, Monday through Friday, 8:30 A.M. to 4:00 P.M. This announcement shall be in effect until Friday, November 16, 1979.

THE MILWAUKEE FIRE & POLICE COMMISSION
Police Administration Bldg., Room 706, Milwaukee, WI 53233
The City of Milwaukee is an Equal Opportunity Employer

This image shows signs of the times in 1979. By the end of 1982, minorities comprised 23 percent of Milwaukee's firefighting force, exceeding the 1974 court agreement of 14 percent. (Courtesy City of Milwaukee.)

Prior to leaving the ruins of a fire during the early 1960s, firefighters examine an area for clues indicating the fire's origin. From left to right are: Gerald Sikora, Richard Davis, Henry Singery, and Lt. Raymond Zbilicki. More in-depth investigation would undertaken by the Fire Investigation Unit, established in 1957. A victim of budget cuts in 1974, the unit would reappear in 1980, only to be eliminated a few years later. (Courtesy Milwaukee Fire Department.)

Large groups of Milwaukee firefighters often participated in local parades. This formation of firefighters, led by Captain Gustave Koleas, marches on downtown's Wisconsin Avenue in May 1965. (Courtesy Milwaukee Fire Department.)

Ladder Company 2's crew begins roof operations at a smoky downtown "worker" during the late 1960s. (Courtesy Milwaukee Fire Department.)

The Bureau of Instruction and Training's long-time Motor Vehicle Operator Instructor, Captain Harlan "Harley" Knem, conducts in-service training on a flood control pump in 1962. Engine 5's 1944 Pirsch is in the background. (Courtesy Milwaukee Fire Department.)

In what has been called an "instant fifth-alarm," the Jewett & Sherman Fire was one of Milwaukee's most spectacular blazes. On May 2, 1967, a gasoline tanker overturned on the corner of First and Florida Streets, creating a firestorm when its tank ruptured. It took two-thirds of the department, with the fireboat and 40 pieces of apparatus, plus more than 50 hose lines, to quell the blaze, nearly 30 hours later. (Courtesy Milwaukee Fire Department.)

Crews worked from a nearby railroad overpass to help bring the massive Jewett & Sherman Fire under control. (Courtesy Milwaukee Fire Department.)

The Milwaukee Fire Department was well represented in the city's U.S. Coast Guard Reserve. Pictured at Milwaukee's Coast Guard station in 1970, from left to right, are: (front row) Jack Karlovich, Earl Tappero, Stanley Gumm, Norbert Detlaff, Robert Callies, Robert Hayward, Gus Valdovinos, and Jim Haight; and (back row) Fred Kohlhapp, Merlyn Peters, Louis Marcone, Lee Forester, Gary Buetow, Dean Wassenberg, and Tony Mikulski. (Courtesy Dean Wassenberg.)

Lt. Richard Seelen teaches recruits the use of fire extinguishers at the Bureau of Instruction and Training in 1963. Seelen went on to become chief of the department in 1986, a position he held until his retirement in 1989. (Courtesy Gustave Koleas.)

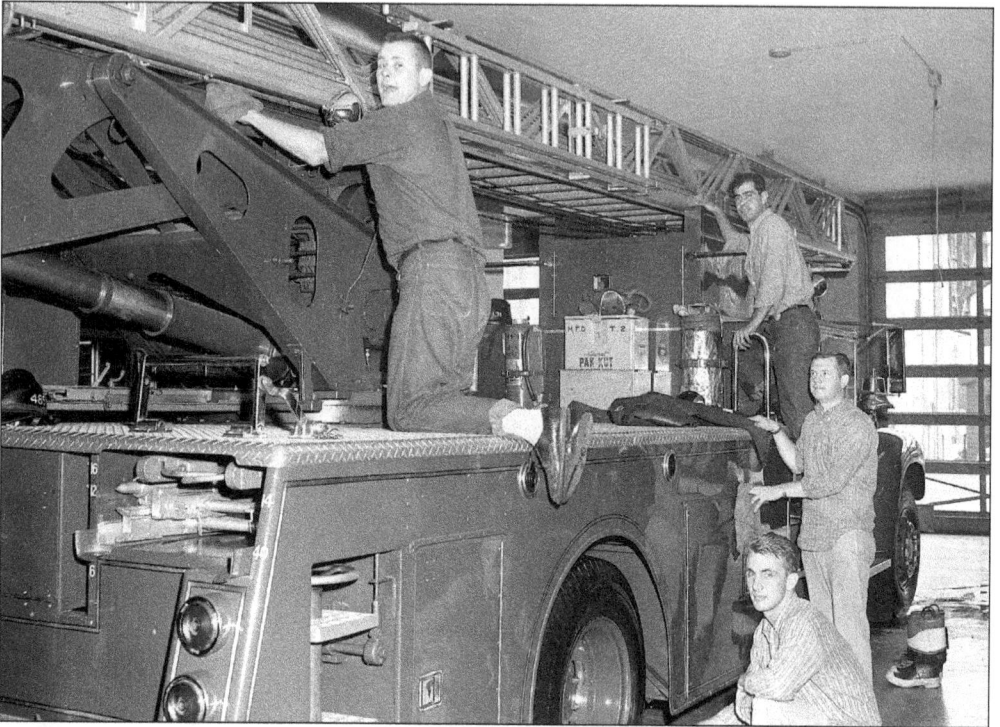

Throughout the department's history, a great deal of emphasis was placed on the upkeep of quarters and equipment. Here, Truck Company 2 personnel in 1965 clean their Mack–Magirus aerial. From left to right, and bottom to top, they are: Leo Kempinger, Richard Rasey, Kevin Clark, and Gale LeFebvre. (Courtesy Milwaukee Fire Department.)

Although members of Engine Company 8 in the 1960s are seen recreating a photo taken in 1910, training sessions in the firehouse remained a common occurrence. Pictured here, from left to right, are: Robert Ballman, Dean Wassenberg, Thomas Davey, Anthony Leiberg, Charles Ryterski, and Gordon Roessler. (Courtesy Dean Wassenberg.)

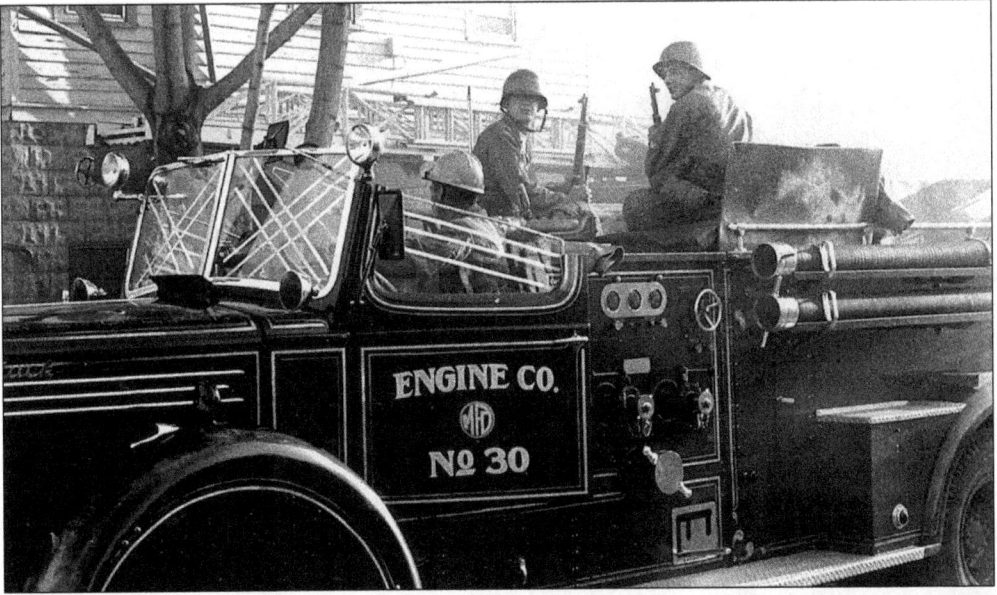

Fire apparatus windows taped to prevent shattering, protective shields, and Army National Guardsmen called in to protect firefighters marked the long hot summer of 1967. Milwaukee, like other major cities, was placed under marshal law to address racial unrest following the slaying of civil rights leader Martin Luther King, Jr. At the height of the riots, fire companies operated as heavily manned task forces to combat a multitude of fires. (Courtesy Milwaukee Fire Department.)

"Big Bertha," a tractor modified with large hose supplying a 2,500-gpm water cannon, was one of many devices used against the blaze at the 40-acre Geipel Dump on the city's northwest side. The stubborn underground fire burned for six months beginning on November 16, 1968, proving a vexation for both residents and firefighters. (Courtesy Milwaukee Fire Department.)

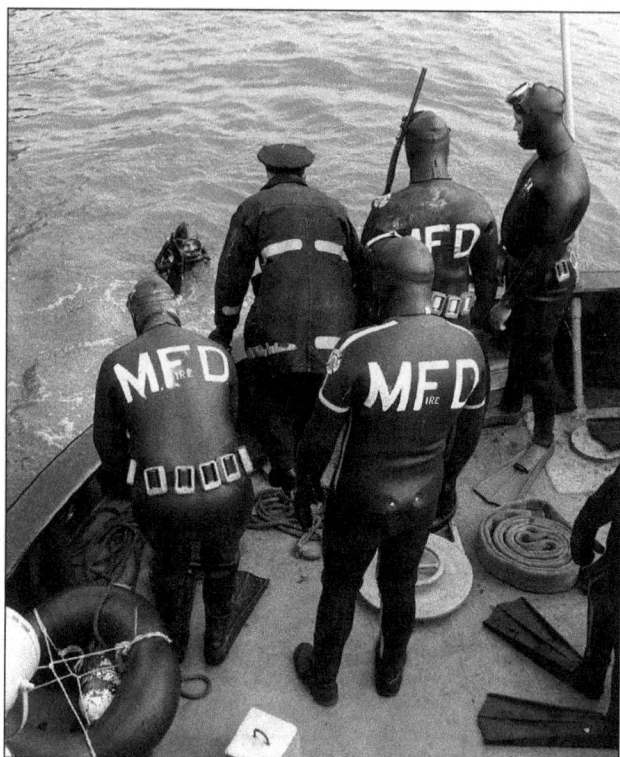

The Scuba Team, now known as "Dive Rescue," is the department's oldest specialty team, having been established in 1962. Bordering Lake Michigan, and home to many waterways, Milwaukee boasts a highly trained and efficient dive team. (Courtesy Milwaukee Fire Department.)

Shown here is the scuba training tank during its dedication at the training school at 930 West Madison Street on October 11, 1968. The 10,500-gallon tank, which permitted realistic scuba training, was relocated to the current Fire Academy site on the city's far north side. (Courtesy Milwaukee Fire Department.)

Concern shows on the face of Firefighter Richard Putze as he and others work to revive a Saint Bernard overcome in a house fire in September 1974. The dog, whose breed is renowned for life-saving, survived, thanks to the firefighters' life-saving efforts. (Courtesy Milwaukee Fire Department.)

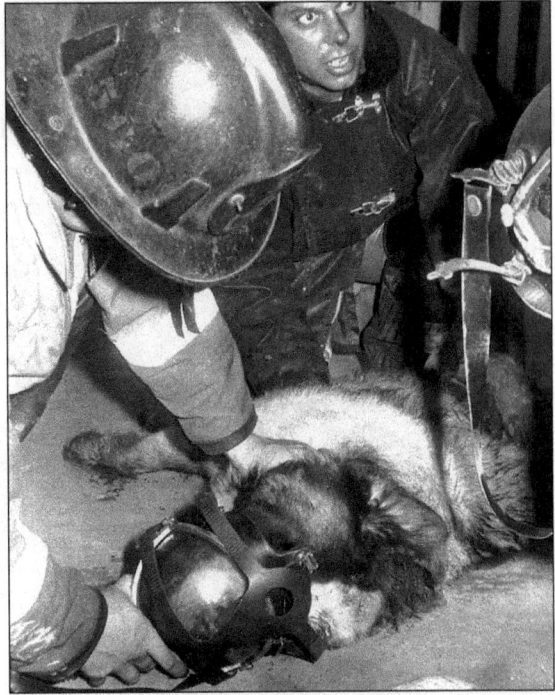

The familiar characters Sparky the Fire Dog and Smokey the Bear are identified as key participants in activities that promote the fire service and fire prevention. Here the pair shares a moment with William Stamm (left), who served as department chief from 1970 to 1986, and Battalion Chief Gustave Koleas. (Courtesy Gustave Koleas.)

Although several firehouses served as shop facilities beginning in the 1870s, it wasn't until 1929 that a shop dedicated to Milwaukee's vast fleet of vehicles opened its doors. "The Shop," seen here in 1978, was built next to Engine Company 3's quarters at First and Virginia Streets. (Courtesy Milwaukee Fire Department.)

Milwaukee firefighters didn't have to wait long to try their new Hi-X (high expansion) foam generator. The unit was summoned to a stubborn three-alarm fire at the Dash Inn on the north side on June 21, 1973. The "Bubble Machine" was deemed highly effective in certain building conditions. (Courtesy King Monaghan.)

This pumper was Milwaukee's only Ward LaFrance, and it was the first diesel-powered apparatus purchased by the department. First assigned to Engine Company 2 at the headquarters station in 1971, this unique rig ushered in a gradual changeover to durable, economic diesel power. (Courtesy Gerrit Madderom.)

Milwaukee firefighters battle a three-alarm fire at Twentieth and State Streets on February 8, 1977. Doss Bender, in the foreground, one of Milwaukee's first African-American firefighters, mans Engine Company 18's nozzle. Bender was active in minority recruitment, and in 1975 was elected President of the Milwaukee chapter of the NAACP. Wearing the white helmet is Battalion Chief Kenneth Hoffman. (Courtesy Milwaukee Fire Department.)

This view of Engine Company 36's pumper illustrates just one of the many hazards faced by department members. While responding to an alarm on June 17, 1977, the engine was struck by an auto, sending it careening down a freeway embankment. Firefighter injuries were severe and the pumper was destroyed. (Courtesy Milwaukee Fire Department.)

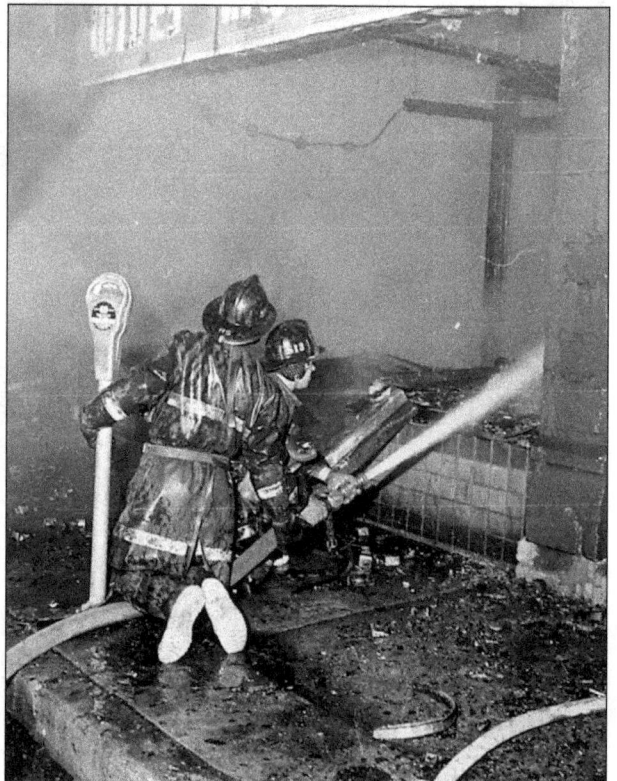

Working against the back-pressure from the nozzle, firefighters direct a large caliber stream through a storefront in the late 1960s. (Courtesy William Mokros)

This widely-publicized image of Milwaukee firefighter Thomas Klatt, of Engine Company 5, drew national attention to the high incidence of fires that ravaged America's urban communities. In 1987, Milwaukee would experience a record 31 fire-related deaths. (Courtesy Milwaukee Fire Department/Ron Overdahl)

Firefighter Bernie O'Connor directs a ladder pipe stream against the massive fire that gutted the five-story Metropolitan Block building at Third and State Streets on December 20, 1975. The landmark played an important part in the revitalization of historic Third Street. (Courtesy Dale Mutza)

The Metropolitan Block Fire was a study in master streams, 25 of which were used. Despite them, and the seven-million gallons of water they blasted against the flames, it took more than 11 hours to bring the blaze under control. (Courtesy Dale Mutza)

Completed in 1901, this firehouse at Virginia and Clinton (later South First) Streets originally housed Engine Company 19, Truck 8, and the water tower. (Courtesy Milwaukee Fire Department.)

Above is the same building in 1971, minus the imposing towers, and with the repair shop, which had been added by 1930. Seen here, from left to right, are: the Emergency Compressor Unit, Ladder Co. 8, Special Equipment, Engine Co. 3, and Wrecker 1. Engine 3 and Ladder 8 remain quartered there, along with updated special equipment. (Courtesy Gustave Koleas.)

These 12 men were the first Milwaukee firefighters to become paramedics. After completing 12 weeks of training at the Milwaukee County Medical Complex, they were assigned on November 7, 1977 to Med 3 at Engine 28's quarters for field training. Pictured, from left to right, are: Terrance Reynolds, Jerome Brukbacher, Robert Bartelt, Thomas Davies, Charles Gauger, Gordon Walsh, Joseph Richard, William Wengel, Jacque Kelsey, John Gutowski, Anthony Mikulski, and Robert Trepanier. The department now operates ten paramedic units for advanced life support. (Courtesy Milwaukee Fire Department.)

Milwaukee firefighters were called numerous times to battle fires at the Sydney Hih complex on Juneau Avenue. This windswept blaze in October, 1976, trapped persons who worked in the building's many shops. (Courtesy Mark Hoeller.)

This image captures the early stage of a four-alarm fire at Twenty-seventh and Vliet Streets in 1974. Engine 32 waits for a water supply, Ladder 9 raises its aerial, and a chief's aide shouts directions. (Courtesy Author.)

The belief of city officials that firehouses should reflect the department's new and more efficient operation resulted in stylish designs such as Engine Company 29, completed in 1984 on Milwaukee's south side. (Courtesy Mark Hoeller.)

Often overlooked is the monumental effort by firefighters to fight fires in common dwellings. Engine Company 13's crew "waits for water" to begin an attack on this fatal blaze on the city's north side in 1973. (Courtesy Author.)

The practice of buying Mack apparatus continued into the 1970s, when the C-95 cab style was replaced by Mack's CF-600 model. Engine Company 9 shows off its new 1,000-gpm pumper at its Walnut Street quarters in 1970. (Courtesy Chuck Madderom)

Milwaukee Fire Academy facilities include this training tower and activities building, the latter resembling an actual firehouse, complete with the school's engine and ladder truck. The main building is a former high school purchased in 1972 for joint fire and police training. (Courtesy Author.)

This patch, designed by the author in 1980, symbolizes the commitment of the training school. The titles "Fire Academy" and "Bureau of Instruction and Training" have been used interchangeably. (Courtesy Jim Ley.)

Under the watchful eyes of training lieutenants, recruits ventilate a fire in a vacant house in 1978. Vacants are acquired in the latter stages of fire training to apply learned skills. (Courtesy Milwaukee Fire Department.)

A fire hose offers relief from training fires and July heat for this recruit in 1978. (Courtesy Milwaukee Fire Department.)

Until the 1990s, few exceptions were made during training in Milwaukee's weather extremes. Members of the MFD learn to adapt to such extremes, for which the region has become known. (Courtesy Author.)

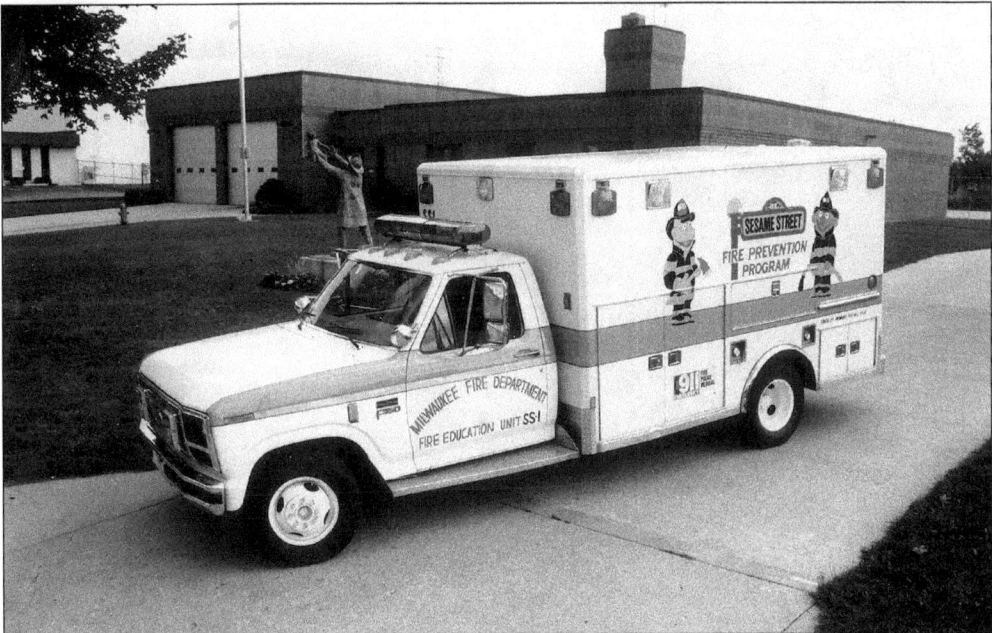

Increased emphasis was placed on fire education in the wake of large numbers of lives lost in fires, many of them children, during the late 1980s. This vehicle was part of a widespread program that included a Survive-Alive house and a public relations corps. (Courtesy Mark Hoeller.)

Using a large hose and nozzle, firefighters of Ladder Company 2 set up their aerial for water tower operations at the Manhattan Apartments blaze on February 12, 1978. The building was located at Ninth and State Streets, near Milwaukee's downtown. (Courtesy Milwaukee Fire Department.)

The trend in Mack–Pirsch ladder trucks in Milwaukee began during the 1960s. The term "McPirsch" was coined to refer to a Mack tractor mated with a Pirsch aerial. Ladder Company 15's 85-foot aerial protected the city's north side. (Courtesy Gerrit Madderom.)

Mack's C-style cabs gave way to the flat-faced CF style seen here on Ladder Company 2's 100-foot McPirsch in 1972. Called "The Big Stick," Ladder 2's rig ran out of the headquarters firehouse, called "The Glass House," which was built at Seventh and Wells Streets in 1961. (Courtesy Gerrit Madderom.)

Firefighters of Ladder Company 10 had just scrambled down their aerial before it was caught in this flashover at Seventeenth and Locust Streets in 1973. (Courtesy Author.)

Engine 30, Ladder 18, and Snorkel 1 are visible working at a two-alarm blaze that destroyed Bohemian Hall at Twelfth and Reservoir Streets on October 28, 1969. Rapid growth of Milwaukee's Czech community led to the construction of Bohemian Hall in 1895. The landmark was the gathering place for the Czechs of Milwaukee for more than 70 years. (Courtesy Author.)

Fireboat 2, called "Roamer," was placed in service in 1963 to navigate the northern reaches of the Milwaukee River. It was quickly discovered that river debris clogged its intakes, prompting a conversion from jet propulsion to conventional propeller drive. (Courtesy Gerrit Madderom.)

During his 28 years in office, Mayor Henry Maier was a staunch supporter of the Milwaukee Fire Department. In 1980, he intervened on behalf of the firefighters to avert a strike threatened over base-pay parity with police. (Courtesy Gerrit Madderom.)

Six

1981–Present

Reminiscent of earlier days, this mural was painted on Engine 32 and Ladder 9's quarters when it was built at Thirtieth and Galena Streets in 1984. (Courtesy Mark Hoeller.)

Fires in waste paper bales plagued the city, and the danger of fighting them was not to be underestimated. Firefighter William Zokan died as a result of crushing injuries he received fighting a fire at the Milwaukee Waste Paper Company on the east side on September 6, 1982. (Courtesy Gerrit Madderom.)

Firefighters and members of Milwaukee's Dive Rescue Team retrieve a person who fell through the ice in March 1984. (Courtesy Milwaukee Fire Department and Brian F. Murray.)

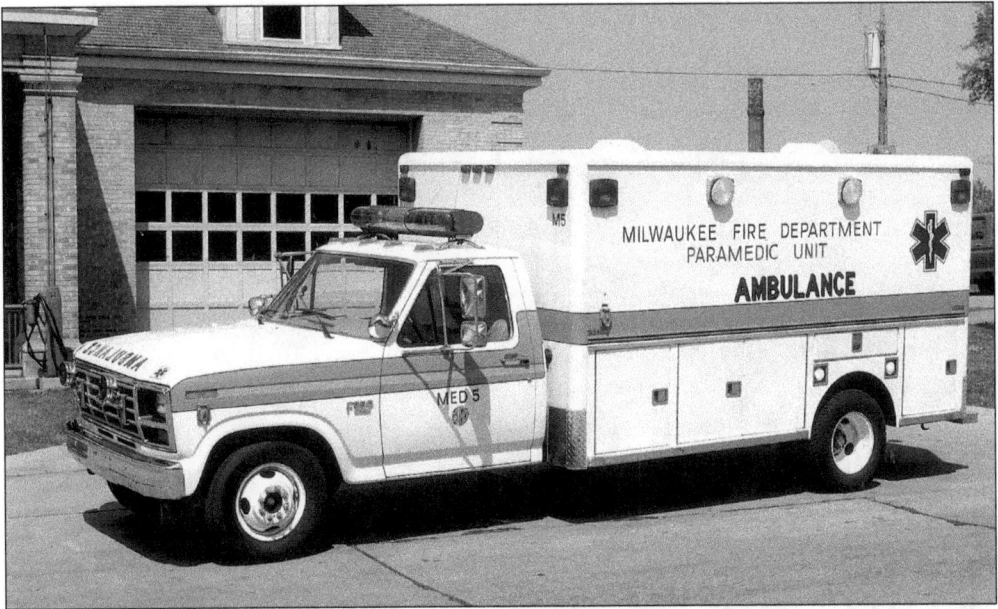

Paramedics answered alarms in modular trucks such as this 1983 Ford assigned to Med 5, which ran out of Engine 13's quarters in the inner city. (Courtesy Gerrit Madderom.)

One tradition led to another in 1988, when the city and county of Milwaukee agreed to provide paramedic service in the congested construction area of the freeway and Menomonee Valley high-rise bridge. Harley–Davidson sold two heavy-duty Police Special motorcycles to the city for $1.00 each. The equipment carried in each comprised a complete paramedic unit. This was the third time in its history that the MFD used Harleys. Some of the paramedics qualified to use the Med bikes are pictured here. From left to right, they are: David Kaminski, Gregory Amos, Jacque Kelsey, James Dallas, Annette Johnson, David Tomasino, Gerald Gifford, and David Jalowiec. (Courtesy Milwaukee Fire Department.)

To preserve architectural heritage, the quarters of Engine Company 27 and Ladder Company 5 on Milwaukee's east side was remodeled in 1988 to resemble the building's original state. (Courtesy Author.)

A five-alarm fire in the school at Twentieth and North Avenue on February 8, 1985 blanketed the inner city with dense smoke. (Courtesy Milwaukee Fire Department.)

When fire ravaged this block-long building complex at Fourteenth and Forest Home Avenue in January 1981, it provided a study in MFD aerial apparatus. From the four types—snorkel, aerialscope, rear-mount, and tractor-trailer—heavy streams were directed against the blaze. (Courtesy Milwaukee Fire Department.)

A changing of the guard is shown here. Ladder Company 18's vintage Mack–Pirsch apparatus is overshadowed by its replacement, a 1988 LTI. The company itself, which was quartered with Engine Company 21, fell victim to budget cuts and was eliminated in October 1988, despite protests by local community groups. (Courtesy Author.)

Chief Richard Seelen (with sunglasses), along with fire department and city officials, poses with one of Milwaukee's 2,200 fire alarm boxes to mark his program for their removal. Chief Seelen instituted the 1987 program in view of the 911 system, and the rising number of false alarms—nearly 15,000 annually—transmitted through the boxes. During most of the years the boxes were in service, "pulling the hook" brought a full assignment, comprising between five and seven pieces of fire apparatus. (Courtesy Milwaukee Fire Department.)

Of 24 women who began training at the Fire Academy, starting in 1978, Debra Pross (now Walsh) was the first to make it through, becoming Milwaukee's first female firefighter. After graduating in January 1983, she was assigned to Engine Company 21 in the inner city. (Courtesy Debra Walsh.)

Firefighters work quickly to get ahead of this fire at Third and State Streets on November 17, 1981. (Courtesy Milwaukee Fire Department.)

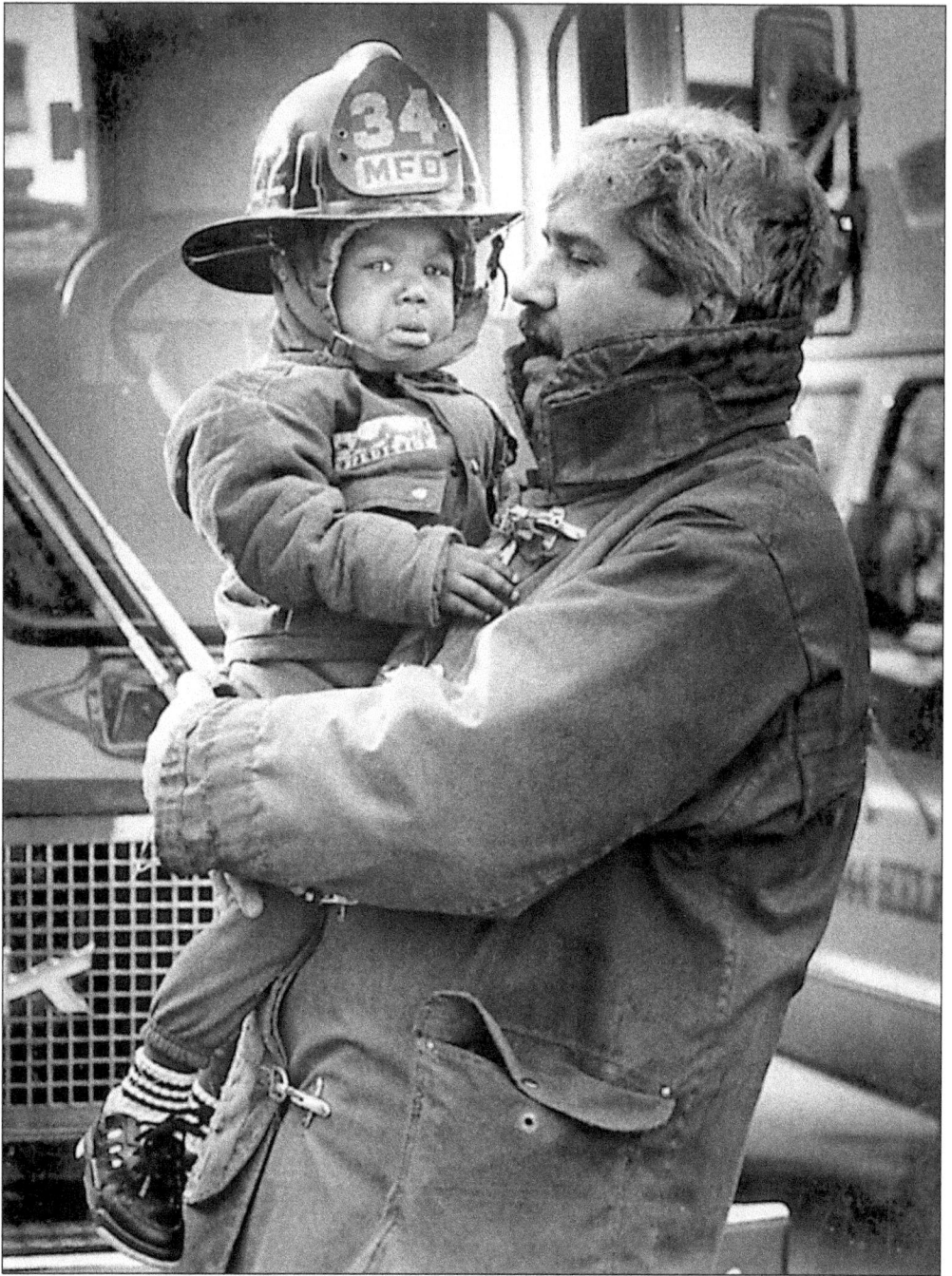

Milwaukee firefighter Charles Conway comforts three-year-old Remington Burage, who was involved in a traffic accident in February 1992. (Courtesy Milwaukee Fire Department.)

The estimated ten-year time frame for construction of Milwaukee's "deep tunnel" project prompted the establishment of the fire department's Tunnel Rescue Team in 1985. The team was put to the test on November 10, 1988, when an underground explosion jarred the area of Sixteenth and Bruce Streets. Pictured here are team members about to enter the tunnel to recover three tunnel workers killed in the explosion. Eventually the team merged with the Heavy Urban Rescue Team, which specializes in high-angle rope rescue. (Courtesy Milwaukee Fire Department.)

Twice during 1981, Milwaukee firefighters, at the behest of their union, went on strike when contract negotiations failed. Parity in pay with the police was the main strike issue. A parity settlement was worked out in circuit court, from whom the city had sought an injunction to force firefighters back to work. (Courtesy Mark Hoeller.)

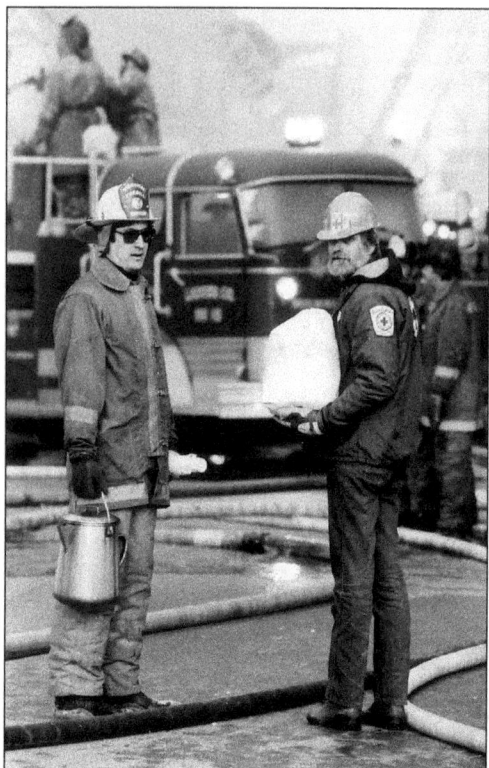

Dean Richards (left) of the Milwaukee Fire Bell Club, and an unidentified Red Cross worker, work the chilly fire lines at Twentieth and North Avenue in February 1985, providing firefighters food and hot beverages. Comprising enthusiastic buffs, the Fire Bell Club has harbored a rich history since its establishment in 1947, and continues to serve the fire service on and off the fire-ground. (Courtesy Milwaukee Fire Department.)

Milwaukee Fire Department's amphibious fire-rescue vehicle is pictured here in the surf at McKinley Beach in April 1985. Originally built for the Army in 1961, the highly modified unit was delivered to the MFD in 1984. (Courtesy Milwaukee Fire Department.)

Firefighters in the aerialscope work on the fire in the Norman Building at Seventh and Wisconsin Avenue on January 12, 1991. The five-alarm blaze lasted two days and claimed the lives of four occupants. (Courtesy Ron Zabler Photography.)

In what is traditionally called "organized confusion," firefighters scramble to contain the blaze in this residence at Twenty-seventh and Garfield Avenue on May 17, 1981. (Courtesy Milwaukee Fire Department.)

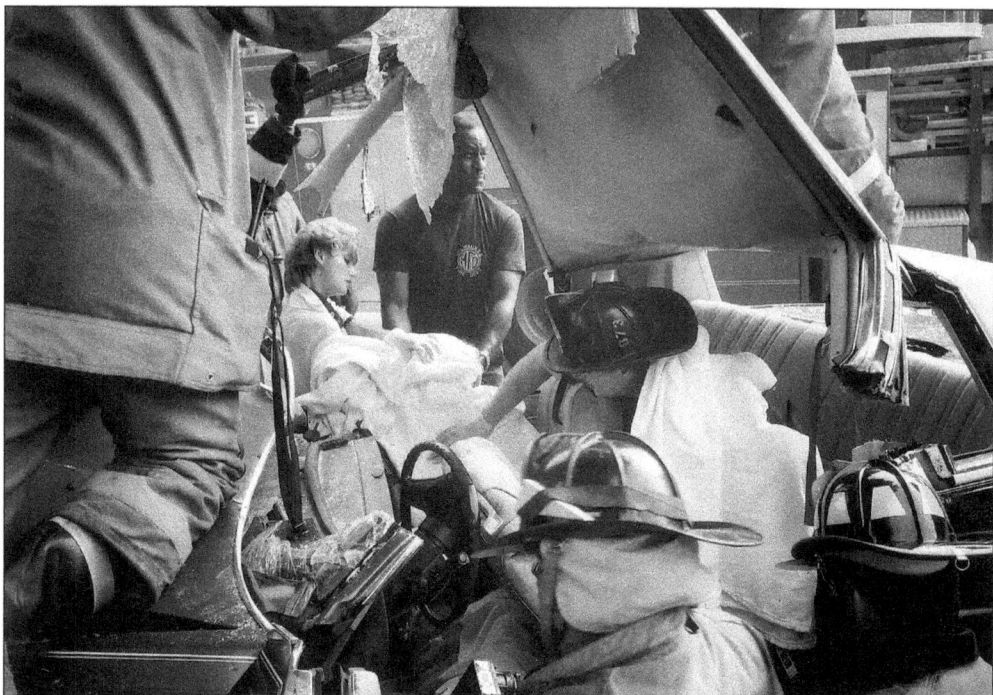

As firefighters remove the vehicle from around a trapped occupant, paramedics treat the person's injuries in July 1994. Since the 1970s, the MFD has been involved with Emergency Medical Services to the extent that nearly 70 percent of alarms are medical related. (Courtesy Joe Kluck.)

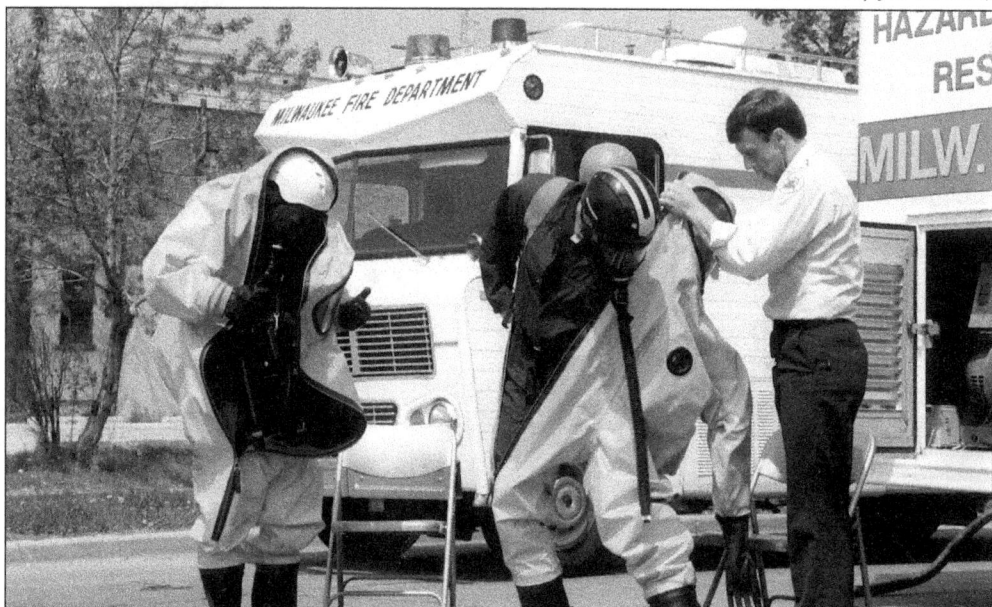

In view of the hazards that offset technological advances, it was only a matter of time before Milwaukee saw the need for a Hazardous Materials (Haz–Mat) Team. Formed in 1980, the team operates from Engine 25's quarters on the west side, and responds to other communities as well. Here, team members don protective suits for a Haz–Mat incident at Fourth and Vine Streets on May 8, 1988. (Courtesy Chuck Liedtke.)

In the February chill of 1989, firefighters battled a spectacular five-alarm fire at Thirty-second and Burnham on the city's south side. (Courtesy Milwaukee Fire Department.)

Firefighters take a breather, literally, following a fire on Cambridge Street on the city's east side in 2004. (Courtesy Chuck Liedtke.)

Fully enclosed cabs and sliding-door cabinets of apparatus began appearing during the late 1980s. Engine Company 1 introduced this Mack–Barnett modification during 1987. (Courtesy Gerrit Madderom.)

From their dangerous position above a fast-moving fire on the east side, a ladder company attempts to "open the roof" to vent heat and smoke, thereby increasing the chance of survival for trapped occupants and enabling hose crews to push into the building. (Courtesy Joe Kluck.)

The Dive Rescue Team put this Boston Whaler, named "Phoenix," in service in 1993. The team's vehicle, along with other watercraft, is displayed in the background. (Courtesy Milwaukee Fire Department.)

The Dive Rescue Team works to rescue a vehicle with a trapped occupant from the Milwaukee River during April 1997. (Courtesy Tom Conrad.)

121

On an inclined roof platform, firefighter trainees learn the age-old method of making roof openings with an axe. (Courtesy Mark Hoeller.)

Nearly axle-deep in water, Engine Company 3's Ford–Pirsch pumper works at a two-alarm fire on South Barclay Street in May 1995. (Courtesy Tom Conrad.)

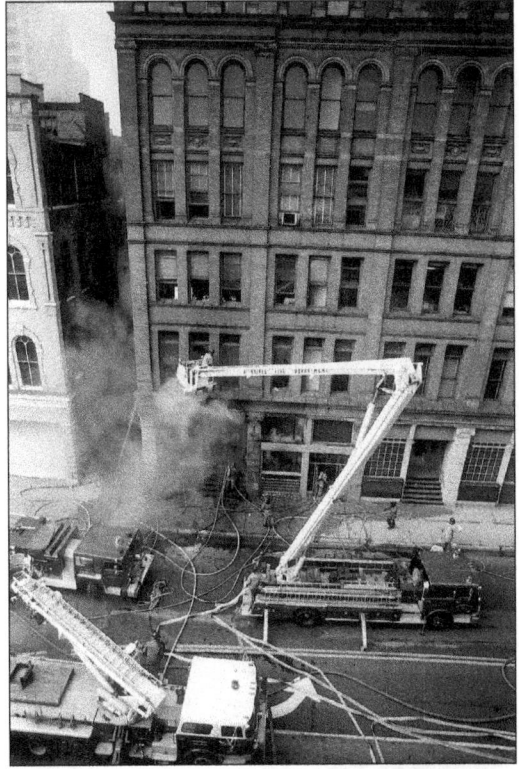

Milwaukee's two elevating platforms work at a fire on Broadway in the city's downtown on April 25, 1980. (Courtesy Milwaukee Fire Department.)

Throughout Milwaukee's history, the Third Ward's produce district, dubbed "Commission Row," has fallen victim to fires. Downtown firefighters work to get this one under control on November 6, 1981. (Courtesy Milwaukee Fire Department.)

Ladder 15's gang ventilates the roof of a burning home on the city's northwest side. Although residences account for the majority of buildings ravaged by fire, and the most injuries and fatalities, they are less likely to receive media attention. (Courtesy Milwaukee Fire Department.)

After cutting a roof opening, a firefighter makes a hasty retreat when the fire vents, as intended. The house fire occurred at Ninth and Locust Streets in August 1994. (Courtesy Milwaukee Fire Department.)

Shown here is the modern look in aerial equipment. This is busy Ladder Company 9's 100-foot Emergency One. (Courtesy Gerrit Madderom.)

Milwaukee fire apparatus has come a long way since open cabs and traditional overall red paint jobs. Engine Company 31's 1998 Emergency One is typical of the large, fully enclosed, red and white rigs that serve the city. (Courtesy Gerrit Madderom.)

"THE LAST ALARM"

Milwaukee's Fallen Firefighter Memorial, located at the headquarters station at Seventh and Wells Streets, presents the traditional funeral procession display of helmet, boots, and coat to pay tribute to the city's 106 firefighters who have died in the line of duty. (Courtesy Author.)

AFTERWORD

In my nearly 40 years of service with the Milwaukee Fire Department, I saw many dramatic changes in firefighting technology, training methods, equipment, and the department's role in the community.

We worked tirelessly to deploy new technologies, upgrade training, secure better equipment, and to meaningfully engage the community in fire prevention, detection, and other facets of fire safety.

I join others in stating without equivocation that the MFD is one of America's finest large-city fire departments, but I can't overemphasize the fact that the department's greatest asset has always been the brave souls who step forward to serve the community in this very dangerous profession. It was my distinct privilege to work with these extraordinary people under very difficult and dangerous conditions. I remember well the countless times we trusted each other, and relied on our training, our equipment, and our leadership—placing our lives on the line to save others.

In my life I have met no more courageous souls or finer people than the members of the Milwaukee Fire Department. Milwaukee citizens are justly proud of their fire department.

—Former Deputy Chief Gustave Koleas

Pictured above is Deputy Chief Gustave Koleas, Milwaukee Fire Department, 1947–1987.